Effects of Social Media On the Way We Communicate and Do Business

Asad Raza

Contents

Abstract

Social media has changed the way people communicate and do business. It has transformed the interaction among individuals as well as among businesses. The social media tools have brought rapid changes in public relations and organizational communication changing it to a more collaborative and interactive system. The use of social media has affected how people communicate and carry out business. The ease with which people can create social media pages and user profiles has ensured an increased number of users over the years. The technology and internet connectivity have opened a new platform for communication making it easy and efficient. However, the online communication face hurdles regarding the data availed as well as cybersecurity for the users. The effect brings about varied speculative and theoretical issues across the academic, business and political fields. This paper emphasizes on the impact of social media in communication among individuals mad also in business. It has been guided by keywords such as social media, social networking, and impact of social media.

Introduction

Social media tools are bringing rapid change to public relations and organizational communication in today's world. The advancement in technology has shifted the internet from traditional consumption-based to a more collaborative and interactive system. This has created new opportunities for both organizational and public interactions. Years ago, when the internet was beginning to infiltrate and gaining hold of the culture, forward-thinking businesses founded their online presence gaining high control over their messages. The interaction and conversations were limited to putting a contact form on the website or an email link. Feedbacks, comments, and reviews were nearly nonexistent, and for them to be viewed by a large group, it meant sending email with subject lines like "check this out," "forward," among others (Gillin 19). Only a small population used internet forums, and the search engines were inefficient. This meant a little interaction in business-consumer communication. However, the case has since changed with today's social media tools presenting significant changes to public relations and organizational tools (Barnes & Mattson 72). This new advancement has brought about the change to collaborative and interactive services hence new opportunities for both public and organizational interactions. Therefore, with the continuous growth of the internet and the increasing importance of social media in communication among organizations, it prompts an investigation on the effect of social media in communication and its usage in business.

The use of social media has affected how people communicate and carry out business. The ease with which people can create social media pages and user profiles has ensured an increased number of users over the years. The technology and internet connectivity have opened a new platform for communication making it easy and efficient. However, the online communication face hurdles regarding the data availed as well as cybersecurity for the users. The effect brings about varied speculative and theoretical issues across the academic, business and political fields.

When social media was initially introduced to the world, the reception was not as high. It was not understood as a communication tool that would later change and influence the way people communicate and conduct their businesses. Today, social media is transforming the interaction among businesses, their clients, and stockholders. Studies show that most organizations use at least one social media platform, for example, Twitter, Instagram, Facebook, and LinkedIn among others. Many companies find it easy to communicate their corporate social responsibilities and sustainability planning through these platforms. Social media has also changed the way employees, consumers, suppliers, and communities communicate with specific brands (Kent and Taylor 36). The revolution of social media has brought a new level of efficiency in communication and business.

Social media is defined as online platforms, applications, and media that facilitate interactions, sharing of contents and collaborations (Palmer & Koenig-Lewis 162). According to Boyd and Ellison, social media is a site that allows individuals to construct a public or private profile, articulate a list of users otherwise known as online friends with whom they share a connection and can traverse a list of connections (227). Shirky refers to social media as an internet-based application founded on the technological ideologies of web2.0 that allows creation and sharing of user's content (19). Social media presents an incredible potential for electronic participation. Social media has four significant strengths; time, participation, enablement, and partnership. The social interface defines the participatory nature of social media. It enables the users to connect, share information, socialize and attain a collective interest. The social media platforms give users a stage to speak and express themselves. It allows everybody with internet connection to cheaply transmit or publish information effectively; it allows real-time publishing of information (Boyd and Ellison 227).

The information paths in organizations are changing from the traditional marketing department activity. Employees in an organization are talking to the customers, suppliers, colleagues through the various social media platforms. The speed at which information travels is beyond the control of the organizations with employees and clients sharing their experiences, expectations, and impression concerning the organizations. The information shared in these online platforms acts as a reflection of the functions and operations of a firm. The power has since changed from what the business wants to relay to the public to what customers, employees, and suppliers say about it whether good or bad (Gillin 20). In the past, companies were unable to reach and communicate with their customers efficiently. However, with social media, they have an opportunity to reach millions of their clients and potential customers, send messages, experiments and get feedback quickly and cheaply. Consumers, on the other hand, can talk to each other, criticize or recommend a product without the input of a company. Social media besides being a communication and interaction tool has played a significant role in shaping the business world.

Research Strategies

This chapter introduces the main components of the research, including research methods and design, while focusing on the research topic area and focus. Research design is the scheme, plan or outline used in generating answers for the research questions. There are various research strategies and designs used in a research paper including quantitative and qualitative designs. In this research, qualitative approach is used to understand the underlying reasons and opinions for deeper knowledge on the topic. Qualitative research strategy gives insights into the research problem and helps to achieve objectives of the research.

The below research will use previous literature to find answers to the study problem. The use of previous literature gives secondary data for the research. It is an effective method as the researcher has the freedom to select the most suitable data for the study. The secondary data will be derived from previous publications from authors that intended to answer similar research questions or similar research topics. The use of secondary data is efficient as the researcher will have a variety of sources to choose. However, it can be time-consuming as the researcher will have to go through many sources to find the most relevant and applicable to the intended research. The materials used will be from reliable sources not older than 20years. The sources will be selected based on various keywords such as social media, impact of social media, social networking, and effects of social media on business and communication. The most relevant material will be selected after reading the abstract to choose the most relevant to the topic. Although secondary sources of data are efficient, cheap and readily available, they are prone to biases. A researcher can be biased with the sources hence selecting those that align with his beliefs. The biasness may also arise where the researcher selects only the sources that tend to fall in line with the research hypothesis instead of selecting which gives comprehensive answer to the research question. The sources may also be published in different languages. However, with the availability of translating tools, the sources can be easily translated into language of choice. This research intends to use the most relevant sources that will ensure the objectives of the research are achieved while answering the research questions. The sources used are peer reviewed journals, books, and other approved publications. To comply with ethical and legal restrictions, the researcher avoids plagiarism by giving credit to the original author where necessary through citation and referencing.

Research Questions

The research questions guiding the study on the impacts of social media in the way we communicate and do business include:

1. What are the most widely used social media tools?

2. What factors affect the usage of social media by individuals and businesses?

3. What are the benefits of using social media?

4. What are the challenges of using social media in communication and businesses?

Rationale for Study

Various studies have been done regarding social media. However, many have not particularly touched on the overall impact of social media in businesses and how it is being used as a communication tool to meet the targets and also as an overall communication tool. Many of the studies carried out on the topic focus on the roles and benefits of social media without touching on the challenges it presents. Therefore, this study will contribute to the available literature on the extent to which social media are being used by businesses and the public and the impacts it presents to the corporate organizations and communication sector as a whole (Gillin 19).

Over 3 billion people in the world are using social media platforms (Hanna, Rohm, & Crittenden 270). This presents opportunities to the businesses and also narrows the communication gap making it much more efficient. Social media has empowered customers enabling a behavioral change in terms of demand and expectations regarding different products and services they get from the business organizations. There is a need, therefore, to come up with a study that will help businesses to better harness the opportunities presented by the social technologies while enhancing the understanding the dynamics and thus increasing the ability to mitigate the challenges associated with social media use.

Purpose of the Study

Despite the penetration of social media in the business and its adoption by companies, the implication of the new technologies in administrative processes and communication has not been well understood. Some argue that the use of social media may alter regular business and communication processes. The usage of social media has increased tremendously, influencing how people share information across the world. However, the impacts of these networks remain pervasive with activities ranging from marketing, economic, educational to social. Organizational are increasingly becoming desperate in trying to understand and embrace social media so as they can be able to come up with more interactive conversations with their audiences and hence be able to react with to the clients' demands. The online presence has created a problem for public relations and thus calls for an intensive study to help deal with the challenges it poses as well as the opportunities in business and general communication (Gillin 20).

The study targets the business communities as social media usage in business has increased over the years. The main objective is to analyze the influence of social media in organizations with a particular focus on the factors prompting the usage of social media in business and communication and the benefits as well as the challenges of its usage in business.

Problem Statement

Despite the adoption of social media as a communication tool in business organizations, the implication of the advancing technology in the business processes and communication is not well understood. This calls for a way to investigate its impacts in business as well as in the communication among individuals. Social media affects the way people communicate and how they carry out businesses.

Literature Review

This chapter reviews previous literature related to the study. The researcher studies what other researchers have done on the same research topic or with a similar research problem, the methodology they used and the success of their study. The purpose of the literature review is to examine previous works directly related to the study. In this section, the researcher studies what other authors and investigators have done regarding the same topic or similar research question. This exercise enables the researcher to know the methodology used in previous works and the success of those studies. The literature review also guides the researcher in determining the theoretical framework used by other researchers. The researcher can also know the overlooked possibilities in earlier studies. The literature review section provides a thorough theoretical framework and understanding of the effects of social media on communication and business.

Social media significantly influences public relations and organizational operations. The advancement has brought changes in the interactive and cooperative services, building new prospects for interaction for both the public and corporations. The continuous growth of the internet and the increasing importance of social media in communication create a gap in research and investigation on the effects of social media on the way people communicate and conduct their business. Companies have tapped into this new offering and have significantly benefitted from the presence of social media.

The usage of social media is indicated by the technological success and overall performances of organizations in terms of communication. The impact of social media displays the authentic benefits that organizations acquire from their use. O'Leary et al. argue that internet usage positively influences companies in various areas such as in the enhancement of Customer Relationship Management (CRM) practices (354). According to Teo and Choo, social media provides transactional and interactional benefits (72). Social media is also critical in business as it improves the performance of a firm in export marketing (Lu and Julian 136). Besides, social media has been a useful marketing tool and has reduced the marketing cost, enhanced customer relationships, corporations' image, and increased the firms' competitive advantage (Molla and Heeks 102).

Social media has made it possible to perform integrated marketing activities effortlessly and with reduced cost (Kim and Ko 167). The brand reputation is among the most critical factor in an organization. Social media has dramatic effects on the brand reputation; it can either enhance it or destroy it (Kim and Ko 171). Social media impacts digital advertising and promotion, improving the value and brand equity. It enhances customer services, increasing innovation ideas and builds customer relations (Solis 153).

The genesis of social media dates back to the 20th century, with the first public use of the word happening in 1997. Ted Leonsis commented on the need for organizations to provide their clients with social media platforms where they can communicate, be entertained, and participate in social environment (Bercovici 20). In the same year, the launching of sixdegrees.com and SNS enabled users to generate personal online profiles and gain online friends (Boyd and Ellison 227). The trend continued the following decade, bringing forth other social media technologies such as social bookmarking services, proper blogging, and wiki-based encyclopedia among others. Facebook and Twitter were also launched in the early 2000s. The adoption of these technologies continued to grow, and social media moved to the mainstream from the domain of tech-savvy (Shirky 19).

The 21st century has seen the development of technology with everything been done in one way or another through technology. In the current world, many devices and platforms have been integrated into the daily experiences to the point that one cannot live without them. When was the last time a person trying to purchase a given product did it without searching it online? This is because the internet is like the second nature of humans. Social media is an intriguing tool that is changing the way people communicate and do business.

According to recent studies, people depend on the internet connection and mobile devices that they believe make life easier. Almost 60% of the population have access to internet connection but less basic needs such as water, gas, and toilets in their homes (Hanna et al. 273). Over the years the hierarchies in the social media market started changing with Facebook becoming the leader in terms of usage. At the moment many people are connected to at least two social media platforms with Facebook being the leading network. An average person spends approximately 66minutes daily logged in to these platforms. The logging, however, is at least 3.5 times per day making a total of 4hours on Facebook each day (Hanna et al. 274). In the labor market, social media networks play a paramount role. Several people have been contacted through social media platforms, or some have applied for a job after seeing it on social media. Similarly, many purchases have been made after seeing and reading ads or recommendations from friends.

The marketing scene is changing concerning interactive digital media. These platforms have empowered customers, allowing them to share, connect, and collaborate, which in turn creates an atmosphere of influence that distorts the way marketers and managers in a firm engage in influencing organizational activities (Hanna et al. 270). Social media platforms such as Twitter, Facebook, Instagram, and YouTube, among others, alter the marketing, promotion, and advertising states. These platforms have seen the changing of the internet from the traditional information platform to one that represents a more comfortable and efficient marketing channel for business. This development helps in reducing the traditional intermediaries and consequently connecting the business to its clients. Hanafizadeh and Behboudi argue that social media has offered an online opportunity that narrows the gap between advertising and sales. Businesses plan to use social media marketing to ensure they are on par with the rest (6)

LinkedIn is the leading and most respected online recruiting network for professionals, although Facebook is the most used platform in all social media market. According to Facebook reports, there are over one and a half billion active users a month. Besides being a critical recruiting platform,

LinkedIn offers the possibility of presenting products, services or brands to an enthusiastic audience. Unlike Facebook and YouTube where original content has to be created thus time consuming, LinkedIn is focused on the content as opposed to the visuals. In a survey in North America on business to business(B2B) by content marketing institute, the most used platforms are; LinkedIn, Twitter, Facebook, YouTube, Google+, SlideShare, Pinterest, Instagram, and Vimeo.

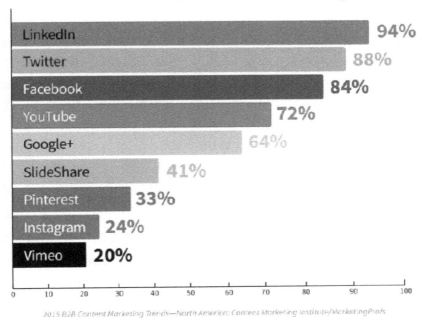

2015 B2B Content Marketing Trends—North America: Content Marketing Institute/MarketingProfs

Figure 1:B2B Social Media Platform Usage

Source: B2B content marketing trends- North America: content marketing institute/marketing profs

The market scene is changing with interactive social media platforms. The platforms have empowered the consumers allowing them to connect, collaborate and share. The platforms have also created spheres of influence that profoundly distorts the way marketers engage in marketing activities (Hanna, Rohm, & Crittenden 267). The social media platforms alter the state of advertising, marketing, and promotions. They transform the internet from a platform of information to an influencing platform that represents a marketing chance for business. This helps in enhancing efficiency while reducing the traditional middlemen by connecting the consumer directly to the business. The social network advertising narrows the gap between advertising and sales by offering online marketing opportunities that are achieved through tracing the customers' reactions (Hanafizadeh & Behboudi 6). Thus, businesses are planning on increasing their social media presence to tap on the marketing opportunities.

Social media has opened up round-the-clock engagement. Firms are employing account managers that manage social media platforms. A look at the platforms such as Twitter and Facebook show that business relay messages even on non-working hours. The use of social media is flexible in time and provides audience with services regardless of the time zone. The smartphone era has changed the way businesses interact with their customers. Individuals do not have to have a computer to access social media; the smartphone does it for them. Business leverage on this flexibility to their advantage.

Social media possess several benefits in the way people communicate and do their businesses. According to Wright, with the increased number of social media users, communication has become easy as many people already understand the employment of these sites, and hence information is easily shared and updated (23). In his study, Crescenzo describes the hardship of gathering information and relaying to the workforce in the past (10). The situation has since changed, making communication much more accessible and efficient. The internet and emails have changed the narrative where one has to make an appointment or make a phone call to pass a particular piece of information.

Kent and Taylor, while outlining dialogic public relations presented the possibility of public relations enhancing dialogues through the creation of pathways for conversations (24). The authors argue that online communication provides a perfect opening for the promotion of dialogues. Organizations can establish relationships with shareholders through deliberately designed websites. In their study, Men and Tsai examined the use of popular social network sites by organizations to facilitate dialogues with the public (27).

Social media platforms provide a source of general information about a company, a way for businesses to interact with the clients as well as with other businesses. The efficiency of communication and information sharing can only be enhanced by improving search engines. When businesses connect with their customers through these platforms, they provide better visualization thus enabling them to make faster decisions regarding a specific brand and even make a purchase. The personalized experiences are ensuring customers have a go-to brand. Small businesses, new entrants into the markets are very active and continuously update their profiles and engage the customers through these platforms. In a survey conducted by consultancy agency clutch on small businesses, it is evident that social media platforms are used to gain customers and maintain their loyalty.

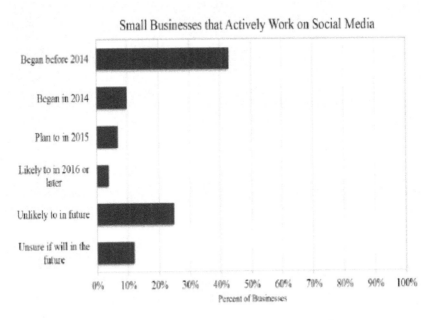

Figure 2:Small Businesses Activity in Social Media

Source: *https://clutch.co/agencies/resources/social-media-2015-small-business-survey.*

In the contemporary world, people spend as much time online as they spend on the real world. A company without social media presence is likely to miss out on the offerings and opportunities presented by these platforms. Facebook presents a huge potential market, and it is becoming increasingly difficult to separate from it. It also becomes difficult to stand out from the crowd. However, the availability of many social media platforms acts as a beneficial tool for businesses as well as for public communication. According to social media examiner in its 2015 study, Facebook enjoys the highest market share.

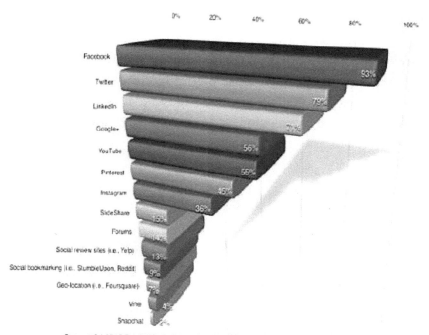

Source: (c) 2015 SocialMediaExaminer - 2015 Social Media Marketing Industry Report

Figure 3:Social Media Platforms and Its Usage

Source: Social Media Examiner-2015 Social Media Marketing Industry Report

The digital era has redefined contemporary consumption transforming consumers into an active group (Liu et al. 600). According to Jones et al., the unique characteristics, interaction speed, machine memory, interactivity and vividness of a company's website defines the reaction of the consumers towards the site and the brand (419). When doing online shopping, a client expects straightforward features from the company's profile. In research conducted by Liu et al., online shoppers give up easily while looking for products online; another percentage turned to traditional methods to carry out their shopping (607). The loss of interest is attributed to engineering issues with the website such as poor design and slow response from the search engines.

As organizations are monitoring their online effectiveness, it is essential to manage their reputation, which is a threat in the online space. The reputation of a firm is at risk and is entirely dependent on social media users. A damaged reputation can cost the company and takes a long time to restore. According to Fuller et al., a favorable reputation reduces consumer concerns concerning purchases, increases consumer commitment and trust towards the company thus encouraging online purchasing (690). Consumers tend to seek third party information and reviews from web sites, friends, review sites and company's social media platforms. According to the social proof theory, people look to others for cues. For new entrants and new clients, trust is built and increases as they see more people carrying out a particular action, in this case online purchasing. The credibility of information also increases depending on the source; an authoritative source tends to increase the credibility which consequently allows the viewer to accept the information quickly. Although third party endorsements profoundly influence online behavior, it does not dictate the opinion of the other party. Companies should ensure to provide correct information and ensure a prominent online presence. A positive experience can easily override any negative review that may arise.

Challenges of Social Media Usage in Organizations

Although social media has presented critical benefits in the way businesses carry out their activities, various challenges arise from its use. Many organizations are often hierarchically structure, and the use of social media may clash with the organizational structure. The new technologies bring with it challenges such as on the norms and behaviors and the level of accountability. Social media being a free space brings about different offerings; as such it may cause distraction to the employees with social networking resulting in low productivity by the employees. Social media can be used to destroy an organization. Although people create profiles using their details, some fake profiles also known as pseudo accounts are created and can be used to tarnish the reputation of an organization. Employers are worried that employees can post inappropriate and hateful information that may affect the organization.

While participating and adopting social media as a communication tool in an organization may seem the easiest trendy way for a business, it is essential to factor in the risks associated with its use. Although social media creates the reputation of a company depending on the positive review from other users, it can significantly damage it. The information presented to the company should at all-time be authentic and credible as false information can cause the downfall of an organization.

Discussion

The research showed that social media usage is increasing in consumers' personal lives and corporate settings. Consumers are becoming more conscious of the products they want and how they want them. Thus, reviews from other consumers and a company's description of a product helps in determining whether clients can purchase a given commodity (Kim and Ko 166 "On the Empirical Study of Luxury Fashion Brand"). The researchers agree that customers appreciate it when they create connections through social media. With the increasing number of social media users, organizations should ensure their increased presence in social media platforms. Customers like knowing that organizations use the platforms to communicate, and they expect the firms to provide them with the required information and options to air their views and comments (Kim and Ko 165 on the Empirical Study of Luxury Fashion Brand)).

From the research, it emerged that Facebook is the most used social media platform. However, LinkedIn leads in professional settings with marketing targeting an authentic audience. Companies have resulted in using social media tools due to the large followership and usage by the customers. The advancement in technology and availability of social media sites in most mobile devices and easy access to internet connectivity are among the reasons for high usage of social media by the public. Some platforms such as Twitter and Facebook have features that allow filtering of information; therefore, companies can configure the settings to fit their requirements, for instance, receiving information most relevant to the organization, thus enabling quick response.

The advantages that come from the usage of social media in businesses influences decision for organizations to involve itself in using social media. Businesses have realized that they can reach to many consumers at once through social media sites. At any given time, many people are logged in to social media sites. An organization can take advantage of this and relay information about the business as well as use it for advertising hence reducing the marketing and advertising costs. The contemporary world is evolving towards a more technologically driven environment. The more innovative an organization is, the more likely it is to have competitive advantage against the rest. Businesses that have significant social media presence are considered innovative and interactive with the clients hence improves its reputation and overall performance.

The research depicts an abstract pattern modeled by West and Turner, which proposes that people understand their needs, interest, and motives and that the audience can make a value judgment of the media content (14). From the results, it is evident that many organizations are tapping into social media use as a critical communication tool within and outside the firms. The review of literature reveals that corporations with social media presence are much more innovative and successful compared to those without social media presence. While many believe that social media can help an organization in terms of marketing and reputation, it is critical to note that the same can significantly damage it. The pressure from competitors is increasingly calling for firms to establish ways they can outsmart their opponents. In such a case, some companies lie and provide misleading information regarding their products and services. The speed at which information shared through social media travels is quite remarkable, and in case of false news, the details reach the consumers at the same speed. Therefore, as much as social platforms are beneficial to firms, it is critical to be wary of such deceptive information.

Social media has been known to cause a lack of socialization. However, it gets credit for helping people to communicate more. Communication is a vital piece in the system, be it at personal level or in business. The availability of social media and technological advancements have made it possible. It is crucial for businesses to keep themselves close to customers and maintain communication. Social media can be used to reach a client and providing specific information tailored to the targeted audience.

Initially, when social media was starting it was more relevant to users for the exchange of personal information and shared interests. However, the dynamics have changed on how businesses communicate both internally and externally. From the study, it is evident that many businesses are taking advantage of social media as an official means of communication. Many purchases have been made online after viewing advertisements or recommendations from other users. However, the deal seems to be becoming sweeter by day with organizations and individuals increasing on social media presence. This is creating room for risks associated with social media. Cybersecurity is being compromised by day, with many people tending to reap where they never sowed. People have been robbed by others whom they thought were genuine businesses. Some create pseudo accounts with similar names to some businesses and known brands using it to steal from unsuspecting users. The reduction in interpersonal communication and dependent on social media platforms creates room for online risks that are hard to avert.

Arguably, social media has generated a total turn around in communication both at personal and corporate levels. In the past, communication was more of face-to-face interaction and sometimes verbally through phone calls. The situation has since changed, with most people preferring the utilization of typed messages. This development has killed verbal interaction among individuals. While it is a more effective communication tool owing to the extensive connectivity of individuals, social media has killed the regular human interaction (Kent and Taylor 35). One cannot gauge the emotions of another individual through texting.

Nevertheless, social media provides effective branding, customer interaction, stronger brand loyalty, and increased real-time sharing of information either from a company to customers or among the clients. Social media and social networking encourage consumers to submit their queries, comments, and feedback, thus enabling organizations to gauge and improve their customers' satisfaction. Arguably, social media assists in quicker access to external knowledge and increased information sharing. While the speed of information is paramount in the sharing of information about a particular product or service, the same pace can be used to destroy the same. For instance, one customer's dissatisfaction with a particular issue can be shared repeatedly across social media platforms, which damages a company's reputation. The speed, although being a win for the organization, makes it hard to rectify a mistake once it gets to the public domain. It is evident that going through social media platforms; one can find a post created year back being shared to date. Although the company can rectify the mistake, the damage is prolonged, with the sharing feature enabling the spread of the same message over and over regardless of when the post was created.

Networking is a natural activity for human beings, but over time, organizations have become bureaucratically structured. The social networks help in re-humanizing the enterprises. From previous studies, technological advancements have made work more accessible. However, how well people choose to use these advancements is what matters. Despite the promising benefits, there are challenges and risks that come along with its use. Organizations are often structured hierarchically; thus, social networks can clash with organizational structures. Companies are also governed by norms and ethics that may collide with the new technologies, behaviors, and level of accountability that existed before the adoption of the new technologies.

Although social media has proved useful in communication among individuals and businesses, it also has some setbacks. Social media gives the users freedom to share everything. Misinformation and vandalism can cause severe legal battles for companies guided by the principle of vicarious liability. The employers and business owners are responsible for negligent acts and omissions by their employees in the course of their work. Every action has reaction whether intended or by accident. Many employers are concerned about the loss of confidential information by a malicious comment or link created by the employees. The loss can result in legal liability, financial damage, security risk among others. Another concern is the tools that social media have whereby a former dissatisfied customer can complain and criticize the organization regardless of when the damage was done hence continuously tarnishing the organization's image (Shirky 19).

Social media has proved to be a useful communication tool among individuals and organizations. The main concern is how safe these platforms are. Many people have fallen victims of social media insecurity. The ease of creating social media profiles and accounts makes it possible for people to create profiles that are used for coning or cyberbullying. The social media sites have no way of verifying the authenticity of an account holder. The information keyed in serves as the only way of verifying a user. Any person with access to a mobile device with an internet connection can access any social media platforms whether with good intention or with malice. Complains have been aired of people using other people's names and brands to create fake accounts. Some people have fallen victims of cyberbullying. Although social media platforms such as Facebook have features for reporting such people whereby their accounts are disabled, the damage can be severe to the victim. Cases of suicide after cyberbullying have been reported. The use of social media comes is not limited to anyone thus users should be careful with their interactions and communication. Some have been trailed from their social media information. However, the security of information, as well as that of individuals, begins with oneself. Gauging what a person posts on these sites and the sensitivity of information shared can help in alleviating online insecurity and cyberbullying. An organization can also establish measures that ensure the information that gets to the public domain is right and does not damage its reputation.

Conclusion

The 21st century has changed the way people communicate and do business. The workplace needs everything that social networking offers. The quicker the organizations realize and embrace technology, the better it is placed in the competitive market. Although social media has been attributed to killing socialization, it has increased communication. In the past although people maintained interpersonal communication, it was not as often as it is currently. A person can communicate with another, miles away without having to travel to where they are. Information is pasted quickly in real-time. As long as a person have reliable internet connection, they will be connected to the rest of the world through these platforms. Businesses have also tapped into this advantage and can reach their clients, communicate and interact thus understanding the consumer needs and the gaps in the market. Social media should be made an integral part of the integrated market strategy for an organization. From the study, it is evident that a large number of people are using at least one of the many social media platforms.

Social media opens endless opportunities from an array of interactions, creating the need to increase studies on social media. Additionally, social media accords users the ability to communicate and make connections that were otherwise unexplored. From the study, it is evident that social media use is on the increase. However, by knowing which platforms and sites to use, a company can hit the target market successfully. It is also clear that for a successful social media strategy, the executive approaches must fully support the idea by increasing the interactions.

Social media is used by more than just individuals. Governments and businesses take advantage of the opportunities presented by these platforms. When friends in the social media platforms like a product, a store, or a given story, the business connects with more than just an individual does; the link spreads to all other social media followers and friends. Although one may deem it as a social connection, social media liking and commenting on particular products or activities go a long way in creating the trust that people have on specific entities. A different kind of trust is built upon the liking or commenting by a friend on a particular product. Social media is an excellent resource for professional networking and for finding information concerning different fields.

Social media opens up whole new opportunities for individuals and businesses by providing endless potentials for interactions and communication. It gives the users the ability to define their preferences, behaviors, knowledge, and communication networks that were invisible in the past. From this study, it is evident that social media platforms elected is paramount. Different social media platforms have different followership and usage. As such, organizations should select that which have large following with the target consumer. This guarantees the successful use of social media tools in reaching the target market. For a successful social media strategy, the organization should enhance the utilization by ensuring it is up to date and with the relevant information for the target market.

Recommendation

As many organizations aim to utilize the open opportunities presented by social media, they should identify social media tools that are commonly used by customers. It is essential to have a business case before making decisions concerning the technologies. Firms should also develop measures that protect the privacy of the consumers, as well as protecting the information. Cyberbullying cases have been on the rise, and this challenge can cause harm to the organizations' reputation. Therefore, corporations should employ strategies that will ensure that customers and all users of the platforms related to these entities are protected.

When adopting new technology or strategy, it is critical to put in mind the likely effects. Social media although providing opportunities for individuals and businesses if misused, can have adverse effects. Blind non-strategic adoption of technologies brews disappointments and eventually failure. Social media can be exploited for the information it possesses of a consumer concerning their intentions and behaviors, it is essential to incorporate social networking sites that not only target the consumer but that which ensures safety for both the consumer and the business. It is vital for organizations with the intention of incorporating social media in their strategies to have full executive support to have maximum impact.

After adopting a new social networking technology, organizations must address the issues on governance that come along with the social media platforms. The organization should set it clear on who is allowed to participate in the activities of the platforms, the rules for usage and the policies governing the usage. Social media brings an array of information that if not well used can cause destruction. Censoring the type and amount of information and organization relays to the public is necessary as it helps the firm avoid issues from the public as well as helping it maintain a clean reputation to the masses.

As many organizations aim to utilize the open opportunities presented by social media, they should identify social media tools that are commonly used by customers. It is essential to have a business case before making decisions concerning the technologies. Firms should also develop measures that protect the privacy of the consumers, as well as protecting the information. Cyberbullying cases have been on the rise, and this challenge can cause harm to the organizations' reputation. Therefore, corporations should employ strategies that will ensure that customers and all users of the platforms related to these entities are protected.

Further Research

Impacts of social media on communication is a highly researched topic. However, few studies have majored on the effect of social media on the way organizations and individuals do their businesses. With the increase in social media usage, studies should be done on ways to incorporate social media in a business plan and draft ways in which consumer reactions can be gauged. It is critical for research to address strategies that would work better for the organizations. Research on which social media marketing tools useful for business is warranted as it will ensure the businesses have what works best for their organizations. Further studies should be done on both the positive and negative impacts of social media on the long-term strategies of an organization. There exists a gap in research with many studies focusing on the positive impacts of social media. Research should be done on the risk of using social media and ways to mitigate these risks.

Works Cited

Bercovici, J. *Who coined "social media"*? Web pioneers compete for credit. (2010, December 9).Retrieved from http://blogs.forbes.com/jeffbercovici/2010/12/09/who coined social-media-web-pioneers-compete-for-credit/

Boyd, D, and Ellison, N. "Social networking sites: definition, history, and scholarship" *Journal of computer-mediated communications* (2007): 13(1), 210-30.

Crescenzo, S. *Is the next Alfred Hitchcock in the cube down the hall? Communication World* (2009): *26*(6), 10-11.

DeLone, W.H. and McLean, E.R. "The DeLone and McLean Model of Information

System Success: A Ten-Year Update" *Journal of Management Information Systems.* (2003):19(4), 9-30.

Fuller, M. A., Serva, M. A., & Benamati, J. S. "Seeing is believing: The transitory

influence of reputation information on e-commerce trust and decision making.

Decision Sciences." (2007): *38*(4), 675-699.

Hanafizadeh, H., & Behboudi, M. "Online advertising and promotion: Modern

technologies for marketing." *Hershey, PA: Business Science Reference (an imprint of IGI*

Global). (2012) doi:10.4018/978-1-4666-0885-6.

Hanna, R., Rohm, A., & Crittenden, V. L. "We're all connected: The power of the

social media ecosystem." *Business Horizons* (2011):*54*(3), 265–

273. doi:10.1016/j.bushor.2011.01.007

Jones, M. Y., Spence, M. T., &Vallaster, C. "Creating emotions via B2C websites [Abstract]." *Business Horizons*, (2008):*51*(5), 419.

Kent, M. L., & Taylor, M. "Toward a dialogic theory of public relations." *Public*

Relations Review (2002): *28*(1), 21–37. doi:10.1016/S0363 8111(02)00108-X

Kim, A.J., and Ko. E. "Impacts of Luxury fashion brand's social media marketing

on customer relationship and purchase intention." *Journal of Global Fashion Mark* (2010): 1(3), 164-71.

Kim, A. J, and Ko, E. "Do social media marketing activities enhance customer

equity? An empirical study of luxury fashion brand ". *Journal of Business*

Research (2011). doi:10.1016/j.jbusres.2011.10.014.0.

Liu, S. P., Tucker, D., Koh, C. E., & Kappelman, L. "Standard user interface in

ecommerce sites." *Industrial Management + Data Systems*(2003):*103*, 600-610.

Lu, V. H., and Julian, C. C. "The internet and export marketing performance: The

empirical link in export market ventures." *Asia Pacific Journal of Marketing and Logistics* (2007): 19(2), 127-144.

Men, L. R., & Tsai, W.-H.S. (in press). How companies cultivate relationships with

publics on social network sites: Evidence from China and the United States. Public

Relations Review.

Molla, A. and Heeks, R. "Exploring E-Commerce Benefits for Businesses in a

Developing Country". *The Information Society* (2007): 23, 95-108.

O'Leary, C., Rao, S. and Perry, C. "Improving customer relationship management

through database/Internet marketing: A theory-building action research project".

European Journal of Marketing (2004): 38(3), 338-354.

Palmer, A., & Koenig-Lewis, N. "An experiential social network-based approach

to direct marketing. Direct Marketing" *An International Journal*, (2009):*3*(3), 162–176.

doi:10.1108/17505930910985116.

Shirky, C. Here comes everybody. New York: Penguin (2008).

Solis, B. Engage! Hoboken, NJ: John Wiley & Sons (2010).

Teo.T. S. H. and Choo. W. Y. "Assessing the impact of using the Internet for competitiveintelligence." *Information & Management* (2001): 39, 67-83.

West, Richard L., and Lynn H. Turner. *Introducing Communication Theory: Analysis and Application*. McGraw Hill, (2007): 14

Williams, R. Inside job. Communication World, (2011): 28(1), 28-30.

Wright, M. "*Moving into the mainstream. Communication World*" (2008): *25*(1), 22-25. Retrieved from EBSCOhost. Rockefeller Brothers Fund, Inc. www.rbf.org.